Needle Weaving
Techniques
for
Hand Embroidery

Needle Weaving
Techniques
for
Hand Embroidery

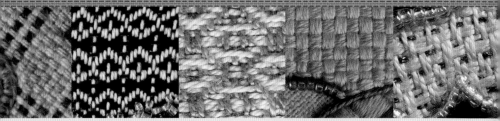

Hazel Blomkamp

SEARCH PRESS

CONTENTS

This edition published in 2017

Search Press Limited
Wellwood, North Farm Road,
Tunbridge Wells, Kent TN2 3DR

First published in South Africa by Hazel Blomkamp, 2015

Text copyright © Hazel Blomkamp, 2017

Photographs and illustrations copyright ©
Hazel Blomkamp and Darren Wilson, 2017

Design copyright © Search Press Ltd. 2017

ISBN: 978-1-78221-517-2

The Publishers and author can accept no responsibility
for any consequences arising from the information,
advice or instructions given in this publication.

Suppliers

If you have difficulty in obtaining any of the materials
and equipment mentioned in this book, then please visit
the Search Press website for details of suppliers:
www.searchpress.com

See more designs on the author's website:
www.hazelblomkamp.co.za

Printed in China through Asia Pacific Offset

BASIC INFORMATION AND TIPS

The basics

- There is one weaving technique on each page of this booklet.

- This guide is bound so you can fold over the cover and pages, exposing only the page that you wish to use.

- By putting a magnetic cross-stitch board under each page, you can use the magnetic rulers that come with the board to mark the row that you are working on, making the instructions easy to follow.

- All of the weaving stitches in this book are variations of the same technique.

- The patterns in this booklet have been divided into three categories: checks and stripes, patterns and textures.

Tips

- Stitch the warp threads first, making sure that they start and end on the outline of the shape. The direction of the warp stitches will depend on what you want from the final weave. It usually doesn't matter with the texture techniques, but techniques that make a pattern, a check or a stripe may need to be placed in a specific direction.

- Leave just a sliver of the base fabric showing through between the warp stitches. If you place them too close together, the final woven area will be too full and may bulge.

- The pattern is formed in the weft stitches and it is in this part of the process that you will vary the basic pattern.

- Tatting thread and Perle No. 12 are the best threads to use when weaving.

- Use stranded cotton and metallic threads to create highlights if you would like to do so, by following the weave adjacent to the line that you wish to highlight.

- By playing around with thread colours, many of the patterns will be interchangeable.

- Use a sharp embroidery needle to work the warp stitches and a tapestry (blunt-end) needle to weave the weft stitches.

- It is almost impossible to create a smooth edge to your weaving. Try to be as even and smooth as you can, but be aware that you will need to either outline the area or cover the edge in some way. Crewel or needle lace stitches, beads or beaded objects and tatting are suitable for this task.

- Once complete, woven areas are sufficiently stable to work simple embroidery over the top – for example, fly stitch fronds can be applied to soften the shape.

HOW TO READ THE INSTRUCTIONS

- Work the warp stitches first. These are long, straight stitches that go from the top to the bottom edge of the shape directly below, following the lines that demarcate the border.

- Referring to 'Warp' at the beginning of each stitch, determine the colour of the thread: decide whether there is more than one colour and, if so, how many warp stitches are to be worked in each of the colours.

- Once your warp stitches are in place, move on to 'Weft'. Determine the colour or colours of thread that you will need to use, and then thread each colour separately on a tapestry (blunt-end) needle.

- Each step number represents a row. Take note of the number of rows in each pattern repeat. When you have worked all of them return to the first row, and then work as many pattern repeats as you need to fill the shape.

- 'O' means go over and 'U' means go under one or more warp threads.

- My experience of teaching these techniques is that, even if you consider yourself to be a 'visual' person, use the diagram for reference only. Follow the text row by row, keeping your place with a ruler. It is really much easier, and you are likely to be more accurate.

- If the beginning of the row has instructions in brackets, you work these stitches only at the beginning. When you reach the end of the instructions for that section, return to and work from the instructions immediately after the closing bracket.

- Repeat the instructions until you reach the end of the row.

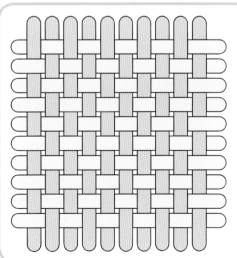

Basic weaving

» **Warp** Colour 1
» **Weft** Colour 2
» O1, U1
» (U1), O1, U1

GETTING STARTED

Warp stitches

- Using the weaving techniques in this book to fill spaces in your embroidery will create the impression of fabric that has been appliquéd on the base fabric of your project. Do not be tempted to follow the shape that you wish to fill. It is important that these techniques are working vertically and horizontally at right angles to one another. Unless you want the pattern of the weave to work in an alternative direction, it is usually best to work the warp stitches over the shortest side of the shape; this is because if any stitches are going to feel at all loose, it will be those.

- <u>Always work in a hoop</u> to prevent puckering of the base fabric.

- Make sure that the warp stitches are taut.

- As a rule, it is usually easier to start in the centre of the shape, working to the left or right, then returning to the centre and working in the opposite direction. This tends to make it easier to keep the angle of the warp stitches vertical.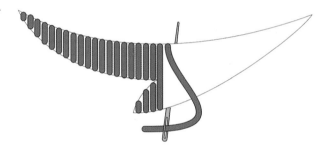

- Use a sharp needle, either embroidery or crewel, to work the warp stitches and leave a space of approximately a thread's width between each warp stitch.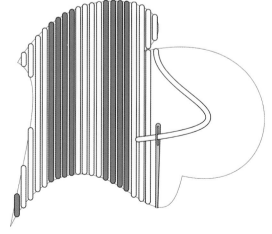

Weft stitches

- The weft stitches are worked, according to each individual pattern, at right angles to the weft stitches.

- It is the weft stitches that create the pattern in the weave.

- Use a tapestry (blunt-end) needle to work the weft stitches.

Textures No. 2 (page 95)

- Always start the weft stitches at the widest point of the shape. This could be at one end of the shape as depicted in the diagram above.

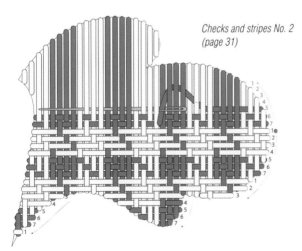

Checks and stripes No. 2 (page 31)

- Or, as is usually the case, it could be in the middle of the shape.

- When working from the middle of the shape, start on Row 1 of the pattern. (See *Keeping the pattern intact* on the next page.)

- Work as many pattern repeats as you need to until you reach the bottom of the shape. The pattern repeat in the diagram above is 7 rows, so you are working from Row 1 to Row 7 each time.

- Return to the centre and work a reverse sequence of rows until you reach the top. This will mean that, in the diagram above, you will work from Row 7 to Row 1 each time.

Keeping the pattern intact

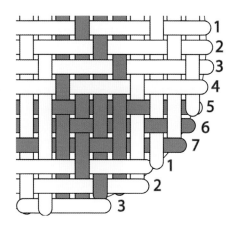

- Having started at the widest point of the shape, you will have to decrease as the shape changes. You will still, however, need to keep the weaving pattern intact; you do this by always counting from the first warp stitch, but only going over or under stitches as they become available. Using the opposite diagram as an example, this should happen as under:

Colour 2

ROW NO.	PATTERN	COUNT	PICK UP FROM
1	(O2, U1) O3, U1	–	Start of pattern
2	(O1, U1) O3, U1	–	Start of pattern
3	(U1), O3, U1	–	Start of pattern
4	O3, U1	–	Start of pattern

Colour 1

ROW NO.	PATTERN	COUNT	PICK UP FROM
5	(U3) O1, U3	–	Start of pattern
6	(U2) O1, U3	(U1)	(+U1) O1, U3 →
7	(U1), O1, U3	(U1)	O1, U3 →

Colour 2

ROW NO.	PATTERN	COUNT	PICK UP FROM
1	(O2, U1) O3, U1	(O2, U1)	O3, U1 →
2	(O1, U1) O3, U1	(O1, U1) O1	+O2, U1 →
3	(U1), O3, U1	(U1) O3, U1	O3, U1 →

General tips for working the weft stitches

- Like the warp stitches, weft stitches should also be spaced about a thread's width apart.

- Weft stitches should be straight. If previous rows cause them to bow, your stitches are too close together.

- When working the first weft stitch, pull the thread straight before going into the fabric at the other end. This will determine where you need to go in on the other side.

- If you are right-handed, always work from right to left, going back to the right-hand side for the beginning of each row. It's impossible to work out where to start if you go backwards and forwards.

- If you're left-handed, work from left to right, it will not make any real difference to the pattern. This will mean that you will have long pieces of thread on the back of your work. So what.

- The tapestry (blunt-end) needle works as the shuttle to guide the weft threads over and under the warp threads.

- Loom weavers use a tool called a 'beater'. It has teeth on the one side that are similar to a comb. This is used to push the weft thread up towards the previous weft thread at the end of each row. You will use your tapestry needle to do this instead.

- When working down, starting from the third row, as you go over and under the warp threads, push the needle up hard so that previous weft threads are pushed towards each other.

- When working in an upwards direction, as you go over and under the warp threads, push the needle down hard so that previous weft threads are pushed towards each other.

- The row that you are working on will always hang down a bit, but you should not be concerned as every row will eventually be pushed into place as you fill the space with weaving.

- If the row you are working on seems to not be fitting in as it should, it is usually because you have made a counting mistake in the previous row.

BASIC
WEAVING
STITCHES

SINGLE WEAVING

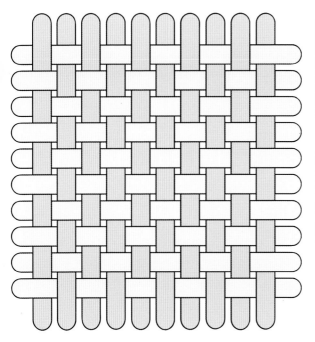

The simplest of the weaving stitches, with a creative use of colour single weaving can be used to create patterns that resemble tartans and checks.

Using slightly different tones for the warp and weft can create interesting effects.

WARP	WEFT	PATTERN REPEAT
Colour 1	Colour 1 (or different colour)	Two rows

» **1**   Over 1 (O1), under 1 (U1)

» **2**   U1, O1

DOUBLE WEAVING

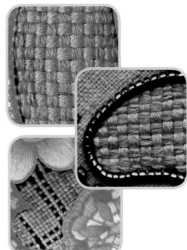

Another of the simple weaving stitches, with a creative use of colour double weaving can be used to create patterns that resemble tartans and checks.

Using slightly different tones for the warp and the weft can create interesting effects.

The use of different colour for warp and weft can give the impression of very small checks.

WARP	WEFT	PATTERN REPEAT
Colour 1	Colour 1 (or different colour)	Four rows

» **1** U2, O2
» **2** U2, O2
» **3** O2, U2
» **4** O2, U2

UNEVEN WEAVING

WARP	WEFT	PATTERN REPEAT
Colour 1	Colour 1 (or different colour)	Two rows

» **1** U2, O2
» **2** O2, U2

CHECKS AND STRIPES

NO.1

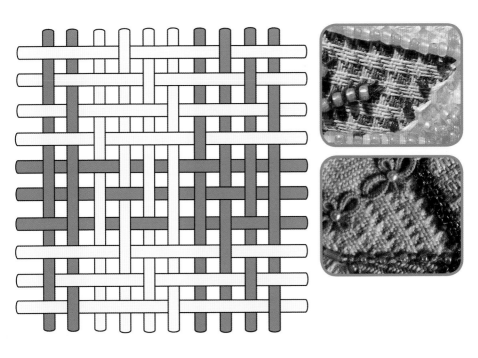

WARP	WEFT	PATTERN REPEAT
4 x colour 1 4 x colour 2	4 x colour 2 3 x colour 1	Seven rows

Colour 2

» **1** (O2, U1) O3, U1

» **2** (O1, U1) O3, U1

» **3** (U1), O3, U1

» **4** O3, U1

Colour 1

» **5** (U3) O1, U3

» **6** (U2) O1, U3

» **7** (U1), O1, U3

NO. 2

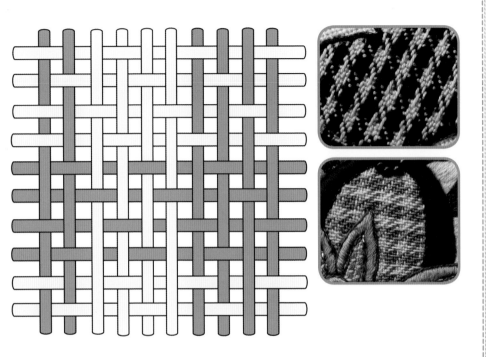

WARP	WEFT	PATTERN REPEAT
4 x colour 1 4 x colour 2	4 x colour 1 4 x colour 2	Eight rows

Colour 2

» **1** O1, U2
» **2** (U2) O1, U2
» **3** (U1), O1, U2
» **4** O1, U2

Colour 1

» **5** (U2) O1, U2
» **6** (U1) O1, U2
» **7** O1, U2
» **8** U2, O1

NO. 3

WARP	WEFT	PATTERN REPEAT
4 x colour 1 4 x colour 2	4 x colour 1 4 x colour 2	Three/four rows

» **1**   O1, U2
» **2**   U2, O1
» **3**   (U1), O1, U2
» Change colour every fourth row.

NO. 4

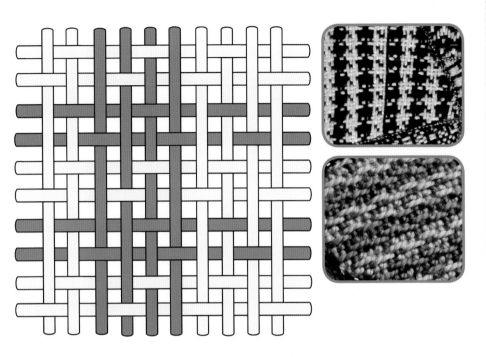

WARP	WEFT	PATTERN REPEAT
4 x colour 1 4 x colour 2	2 x colour 1 2 x colour 2	Four rows

Colour 1

» **1** (U2) O1, U2
» **2** O1, U2

Colour 2

» **3** (U2) O1, U2
» **4** (U1) O1, U2

NO. 5

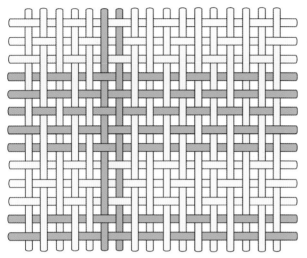

WARP	WEFT	PATTERN REPEAT
10 x colour 1 2 x colour 2	5 x colour 2 3 x colour 1	Eight rows

Colour 1

» **1** (U1) O1, U2
» **2** O1, U2
» **3** (U1) O1, U2

Colour 2

» **4** (U2) O1, U2
» **5** O1, U1
» **6** (U1) O1, U1
» **7** O1, U1
» **8** (U2) O1, U2

NO. 6

WARP	WEFT	PATTERN REPEAT
Colour 1	Colour 1 Colour 2	Ten rows

Colour 1

» **1** O1, U1
» **2** U1, O1

Colour 2

» **3** O3, U1
» **4** (O1, U1) O3, U1
» **5** O3, U1

Colour 1

» **6** U1, O1
» **7** O1, U1

Colour 2

» **8** (U1) O3, U1
» **9** (O2, U1) O3, U1
» **10** (U1) O3, U1

NO. 7

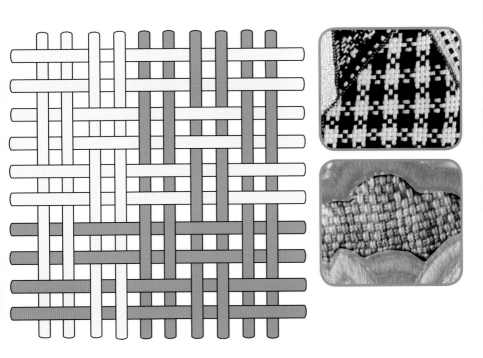

WARP	WEFT	PATTERN REPEAT
6 x colour 1 6 x colour 2	6 x colour 1 6 x colour 2	Twelve rows

Colour 1

- » **1** O2, U2
- » **2** O2, U2
- » **3** (U2) O2, U2
- » **4** (U2) O2, U2
- » **5** O2, U2
- » **6** O2, U2

Colour 2

- » **7** (U2) O2, U2
- » **8** (U2) O2, U2
- » **9** O2, U2
- » **10** O2, U2
- » **11** (U2) O2, U2
- » **12** (U2) O2, U2

NO. 8

WARP	WEFT	PATTERN REPEAT
4 x colour 1 4 x colour 2	4 x colour 1 4 x colour 2	Eight rows

Colour 1

» **1** (U2) O2, U2
» **2** (U2) O2, U2
» **3** O2, U2
» **4** O2, U2

Colour 2

» **5** (U2) O2, U2
» **6** (U2) O2, U2
» **7** O2, U2
» **8** O2, U2

NO. 9

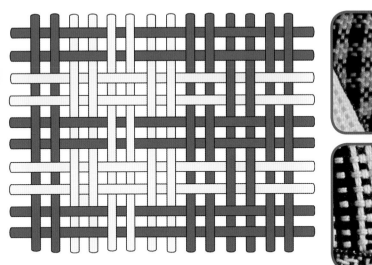

WARP	WEFT	PATTERN REPEAT
6 x colour 1 6 x colour 2	2 x colour 1 2 x colour 2	Four rows

Colour 1

» **1** (U2) O2, U2

» **2** (U2) O2, U2

Colour 2

» **3** O2, U2

» **4** O2, U2

NO. 10

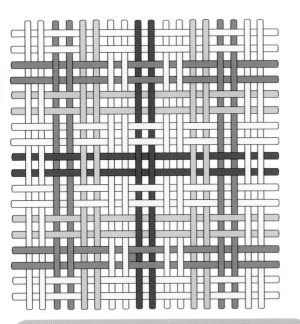

This technique is an example of a check pattern made with double weaving, and can be varied to suit your taste.

PATTERN REPEAT	COLOUR THREADS
Eight rows	Four different colours

Warp

- » **1** 2 x colour 1
- » **2** *2 x colour 2
- » **3** 2 x colour 3
- » **4** 2 x colour 1
- » **5** 2 x colour 4
- » **6** 2 x colour 1
- » **7** 2 x colour 3
- » **8** 2 x colour 2
- » **9** 2 x colour 1*
- » Repeat * to *

Weft

- » **1** 2 x colour 1 – (U2) O2, U2 for two rows
- » **2** 2 x colour 2 – **O2, U2 for two rows
- » **3** 2 x colour 3 – (U2) O2, U2 for two rows
- » **4** 2 x colour 1 – O2, U2 for two rows
- » **5** 2 x colour 4 – (U2) O2, U2 for two rows
- » **6** 2 x colour 1 – O2, U2 for two rows
- » **7** 2 x colour 3 – (U2) O2, U2 for two rows
- » **8** 2 x colour 2 – O2, U2 for two rows
- » **9** 2 x colour 1 – (U2) O2, U2 for two rows**
- » Repeat ** to **

NO. 11

This technique is an example of a check pattern made with single weaving, and can be varied to suit your taste.

PATTERN REPEAT	COLOUR THREADS
Seventeen rows	Five different colours

Warp

- » **1** 2 x colour 1
- » **2** *1 x colour 2
- » **3** 1 x colour 3
- » **4** 1 x colour 1
- » **5** 3 x colour 4
- » **6** 2 x colour 5
- » **7** 3 x colour 4
- » **8** 1 x colour 2
- » **9** 1 x colour 3
- » **10** 1 x colour 1*
- » Repeat * to *

Weft

- » **1** Colour 1 – O1, U1
- » **2** **Colour 1 – (U1) O1, U1
- » **3** Colour 2 – O1, U1
- » **4** Colour 3 – (U1) O1, U1
- » **5** Colour 2 – O1, U1
- » **6** Colour 4 – (U1) O1, U1
- » **7** Colour 4 – O1, U1
- » **8** Colour 4 – (U1) O1, U1
- » **9** Colour 5 – O1, U1
- » **10** Colour 5 – (U1) O1, U1
- » **11** Colour 4 – O1, U1
- » **12** Colour 4 – (U1) O1, U1
- » **13** Colour 4 – O1, U1
- » **14** Colour 2 – (U1) O1, U1
- » **15** Colour 3 – O1, U1
- » **16** Colour 2 – (U2) O1, U1
- » **17** Colour 1 – O1, U1**
- » Repeat ** to **

NO. 12

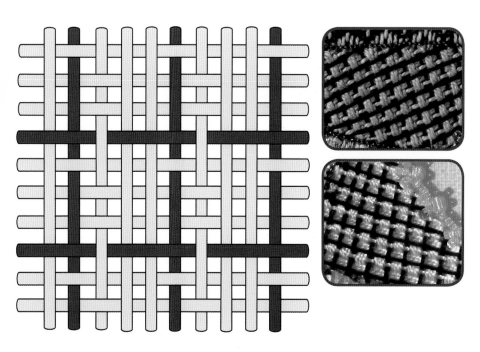

WARP	WEFT	PATTERN REPEAT
1 x colour 1 3 x colour 2	3 x colour 2 1 x colour 1	Four rows

Colour 2

» **1** O1, U3

» **2** (U3) O1, U3

» **3** (U3) O1, U3

Colour 1

» **4** O3, U1

NO. 13

WARP	WEFT	PATTERN REPEAT
Colour 1	Colour 2 Colour 3	Four rows

Colour 2

» **1** (U2) O2, U2
» **2** (U2) O2, U2

Colour 3

» **3** O2, U2
» **4** O2, U2

NO. 14

WARP	WEFT	PATTERN REPEAT
Colour 1	Colour 2	Six rows

- » **1** O1, U3
- » **2** O2, U2
- » **3** O3, U1
- » **4** (U3) O1, U3
- » **5** (U2) O2, U2
- » **6** (U1) O3, U1

NO. 15

WARP	WEFT	PATTERN REPEAT
3 x colour 1 3 x colour 2	5 x colour 2 1 x colour 1	Six rows

Colour 2

- » **1** O3, U3
- » **2** O1, U1
- » **3** O3, U3
- » **4** (U1) O1, U1
- » **5** (U3) O3, U3

Colour 1

- » **6** (U1) O1, U1

PATTERNS

NO. 1

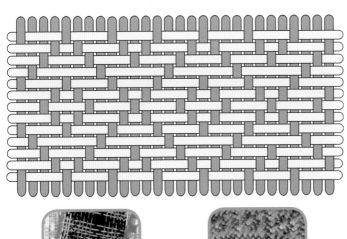

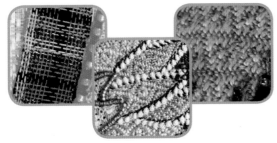

WARP	WEFT	PATTERN REPEAT
Colour 1	Colour 2	Twelve rows

» **1** O3, U1

» **2** (U1) O3, U1, O1, U1

» **3** (O1, U1) O3, U1

» **4** (O2, U1) O5, U1

» **5** O3, U1

» **6** (U1) O3, U1, O1, U1

» **7** (O1, U1) O3, U1

» **8** (U1) O3, U1, O1, U1

» **9** O3, U1

» **10** (O2, U1) O5, U1

» **11** (O1, U1) O3, U1

» **12** (U1) O3, U1, O1, U1

NO. 2

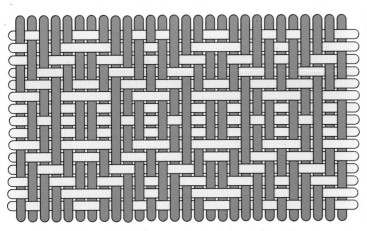

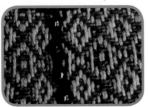

WARP	WEFT	PATTERN REPEAT
Colour 1	Colour 2	Fourteen rows

» **1** (O1, U3) O1, U1, O1, U3, O2, U3

» **2** (O2, U3) O1, U3, O4, U3

» **3** (U1) O2, U2, O1, U2, O2, U2

» **4** (U2) O2, U3, O2, U4

» **5** (O1, U2) O2, U1, O2, U2, O2, U2

» **6** (O2, U2) O3, U2, O4, U2

» **7** (U1) O1, U3, O1, U3, O1, U2

» **8** (U1) O1, U1, O1, U1, O1, U1, O1, U1, O1, U2

» **9** Repeat Row 7

» **10** Repeat Row 6

» **11** Repeat Row 5

» **12** Repeat Row 4

» **13** Repeat Row 3

» **14** Repeat Row 2

NO. 3

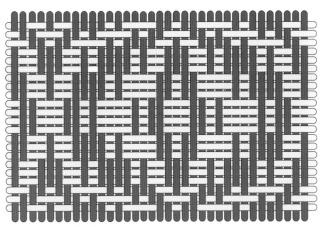

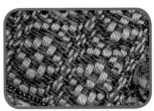

WARP	WEFT	PATTERN REPEAT
Colour 1	Colour 2	Twenty-one rows

» **1** (U1) O2, U4, O1, U1, O4, U2, O1, U2, O4, U1, O1, U4, O2, U1

» **2** (O2, U2) O1, U1, O4, U1, O1, U2, O3, U2, O1, U1, O4, U1, O1, U2, O3, U2

» **3** O1, U2, O4, U1, O1, U4, O2, U1, O2, U4, O1, U1, O4, U2

» **4** *(U2) O2, U1, O1, U4, O1, U1, O2, U3, O2, U1, O1, U4, O1, U1, O2, U3*

» **5** Repeat * to *

» **6** Repeat * to *

» **7** #(U1) O2, U4, O1, U1, O4, U2, O1, U2, O4, U1, O1, U4, O2, U1#

» **8** Repeat # to #

» **9** Repeat # to #

» **10** «(O2, U2) O1, U1, O4, U1, O1, U2, O3, U2, O1, U1, O4, U1, O1, U2, O3, U2»

» **11** Repeat « to »

» **12** Repeat « to »

» **13** Repeat « to »

» **14** Repeat Row 7 (#)

» **15** Repeat Row 8 (#)

» **16** Repeat Row 9 (#)

» **17** Repeat Row 4 (*)

» **18** Repeat Row 5 (*)

» **19** Repeat Row 6 (*)

» **20** Repeat Row 3

» **21** Repeat Row 2

NO. 4

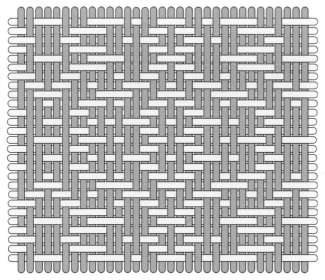

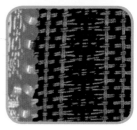

WARP	WEFT	PATTERN REPEAT
Colour 1	Colour 2	Twenty-two rows

» **1** O3, U3, O4, U1, O1, U2, O3, U2, O1, U1, O4, U3

» **2** (U4) O4, U5, O2, U1, O2, U5, O4, U5

» **3** (U3) O2, U5, O1, U1, O2, U3, O2, U1, O1, U5, O2, U3

» **4** (U4) O4, U5, O2, U1, O2, U5, O4, U5

» **5** O3, U3, O4, U4, O3, U4, O4, U3

» **6** (U4) O4, U5, O2, U1, O2, U5, O4, U5

» **7** (U3) O2, U4, O1, U2, O2, U3, O2, U2, O1, U4, O2, U3

» **8** (O1, U1) O2, U2, O1, U3, O3, U2, O1, U2, O3, U3, O1, U2, O2, U1

» **9** O3, U4, O4, U3, O3, U3, O4, U4

» **10** (U1) O1, U3, O3, U1, O1, U3, O2, U1, O2, U3, O1, U1, O3, U3

» **11** (U4) O2, U6, O2, U3, O2, U6, O2, U5

» **12** (U3) O2, U3, O1, U1, O3, U2, O1, U2, O3, U1, O1, U3, O2, U3

» **13** (U4) O2, U6, O2, U3, O2, U6, O2, U5

» **14** O3, U2, O3, U1, O1, U3, O2, U1, O2, U3, O1, U1, O3, U2

» **15–22** Repeat each row in the following order: 13, 12, 11, 10, 9, 8, 7 and 6

NO. 5

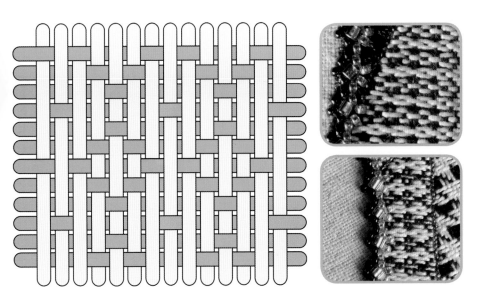

WARP	WEFT	PATTERN REPEAT
Colour 1	Colour 2	Six rows

- » **1** (U1) O1, U3, O1, U1
- » **2** (U2) O1, U1, O1, U3
- » **3** (U3) O1, U5
- » **4** O1, U5
- » **5** (U3) O1, U5
- » **6** (U2) O1, U1, O1, U3

NO. 6

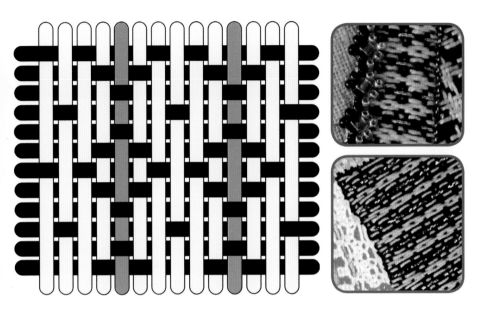

WARP	WEFT	PATTERN REPEAT
5 x colour 1 1 x colour 2	Colour 3	Six rows

» **1** (U1, O1, U1) O1, U3, O1, U1

» **2** O1, U3, O1, U1

» **3** (U5) O1, U5

» **4** (U2) O1, U5

» **5** (U5) O1, U5

» **6** O1, U3, O1, U1

NO. 7

Please turn to page 75 to view the stitch diagram.

WARP	WEFT
Colour 1	Colour 1
	Colour 2

Colour 2

» **1** (O2, U1) O1, U1, O1, U1, O3, U1, O1, U1, O1, U1, O1, U1, O3, U1

» **2** (U1) O1, U2, O1, U2, O1, U1, O1, U2, O1, U1, O1, U2, O1, U1, O1, U2, O1, U2, O1, U1, O1, U2, O1, U2, O1, U1

» **3** (O2, U1) O1, U1, O1, U1, O3, U1, O1, U3, O1, U1, O3, U1, O1, U1, O1, U1, O3, U1

» **4** (U2, O1, U1, O1, U1, O1, U3, O1, U2,) O1, U2, O1, U3, O1, U1, O1, U1, O1, U3, O1, U1, O1, U1, O1, U3, O1, U2

» **5** (U1) O1, U1, O1, U1, O1, U1, O1, U1, O1, U2, O3, U2, O1, U1, O1, U1, O1, U1, O1, U1, O1, U1

» **6** O1, U1, O1, U1, O1, U1, O1, U1, O1, U4, O1, U4, O1, U1, O1, U1, O1, U1, O1, U1

Colour 1

» **7** (U1) O1, U1

Colour 2

» **8** O1, U1, O1, U1, O1, U1, O1, U2, O2, U2, O1, U2, O2, U2, O1, U1, O1, U1, O1, U1, O1, U1

» **9** (O1, U2) O2, U1, O1, U1, U5, O3, U5, O1, U1, O2, U2, O1, U2

» **10** (U2) O3, U1, O1, U1, O1, U2, O5, U2, O1, U1, O1, U1, O3, U3

» **11** O1, U4, O2, U1, O1, U1, O3, U1, O3, U1, O1, U1, O2, U4

» **12** (U2) O5, U1, O1, U1, O3, U1, O3, U1, O1, U1, O5, U3

» **13** O1, U6, O2, U1, O1, U2, O1, U2, O1, U1, O2, U6

» **14** (U1) O1, U2, O5, U4, O1, U4, O5, U2, O1, U1

» **15** O1, U1, O1, U6, O2, U1, O3, U1, O2, U6, O1, U1

» **16** U1, O1, U1, O1, U1, O3, U1, O2, U1, O3, U1, O2, U1, O3, U1, O1, U1, O3

» **17** O1, U3, O3, U4, O1, U3, O1, U4, O3, U3

» **18** (U3) O4, U2, O2, U1, O3, U1, O2, U2, O4, U5

» **19** O1, U1, O3, U2, O4, U1, O1, U1, O1, U1, O4, U2, O3, U1

» **20–31** Repeat each row in the following order: 19, 18, 17, 16, 15, 14, 13, 12, 11, 10, 9 and 8

Colour 1

» **32** Repeat Row 7

Colour 2

» **33–37** Repeat each row in the following order: 6, 5, 4, 3 and 2

» Back to Row 1

NO. 8

 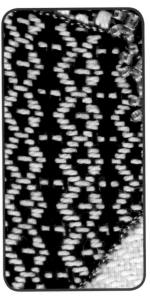

WARP	WEFT	PATTERN REPEAT
Colour 1	Colour 2	Seventeen rows

» **1** (U1) O1, U3

» **2** (U4) O3, U5

» **3** (U3) O2, U1, O2, U3

» **4** (O1) U1, O3

» **5** (O4) U3, O5

» **6** (U3) O5, U3

» **7** (U3) O5, U3

» **8** (O4) U3, O5

» **9** (O1) U1, O3

» **10** (U3) O2, U1, O2, U3

» **11** (U4) O3, U5

» **12** (U1) O1, U3

» **13** O3, U5

» **14** (O1) U1, O2, U3, O2

» **15** (O1, U1) O3, U1

» **16** (O1) U1, O2, U3, O2

» **17** O3, U5

NO. 9 – MUSIC STAVES

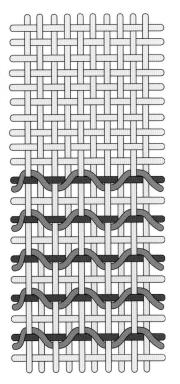

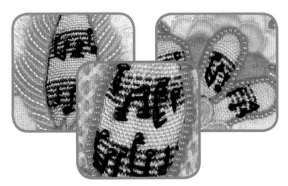

WARP	WEFT	PATTERN REPEAT
Colour 1 (Perle No.12)	Colour 1 (Perle No. 12) Colour 2 (Single strand, stranded cotton)	Twenty-four rows

Once you have completed the staves, stitch the music notes using a thread that is a shade darker than the one you used for the lines. Use either French knots or size 15° beads for the dots and straight stitches for the lines.

Colour 1

» **1** U1, O1
» **2** O1, U1
» **3** U1, O1
» **4** O1, U1
» **5** U1, O1
» **6** O1, U1
» **7** U1, O1
» **8** O1, U1
» **9** U1, O1
» **10** O1, U1

Colour 2

» **11** U1, O1
» **12** U1 (behind), O1 (front)

Colour 1

» **13** O1, U1

Colour 2

» **14** U1, O1
» **15** U1 (behind), O1 (front)

Colour 1

» **16** O1, U1

Colour 2

» **17** U1, O1
» **18** U1 (behind), O1 (front)

Colour 1

» **19** O1, U1

Colour 2

» **20** U1, O1
» **21** U1 (behind), O1 (front)

Colour 1

» **22** O1, U1

Colour 2

» **23** U1, O1
» **24** U1 (behind), O1 (front)

» Return to Row 1

NO. 10 – BRAIDS & EDGES

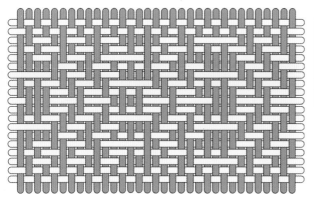

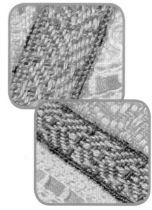

WARP	WEFT
Colour 1 (12mm (½in) stitches)	2 x colour 1 15 x colour 2 2 x colour 1

Using Perle No. 12 thread, this weave covers a height of 12mm (½in), with the length being as wide as you need.

Colour 1

» **1** U1, O1

» **2** O1, U1

Colour 2

» **3** (U1) O2, U4, O1, U1, O4, U2, O1, U2, O4, U1, O1, U4, O2, U1

» **4** (O2, U2) O1, U1, O4, U1, O1, U2, O3, U2, O1, U1, O4, U1, O1, U2, O3, U2

» **5** O1, U2, O4, U1, O1, U4, O2, U1, O2, U4, O1, U1, O4, U2

» **6** *(U2) O2, U1, O1, U4, O1, U1, O2, U3, O2, U1, O1, U4, O1, U1, O2, U3*

» **7** Repeat * to *

» **8** Repeat * to *

» **9** #(U1) O2, U4, O1, U1, O4, U2, O1, U2, O4, U1, O1, U4, O2, U1#

» **10** Repeat # to #

» **11** Repeat # to #

» **12** «(O2, U2) O1, U1, O4, U1, O1, U2, O3, U2, O1, U1, O4, U1, O1, U2, O3, U2»

» **13** Repeat « to »

» **14** Repeat « to »

» **15** Repeat « to »

» **16** Repeat Row 11 (#)

» **17** Repeat Row 10 (#)

» **18** Repeat Row 9 (#)

» **19** Repeat Row 8 (*)

» **20** Repeat Row 7 (*)

» **21** Repeat Row 6 (*)

» **22** Repeat Row 5

» **23** Repeat Row 4

» **24** Repeat Row 3

Colour 1

» **25** Repeat Row 2

» **26** Repeat Row 1

NO. 11 – BRAIDS & EDGES

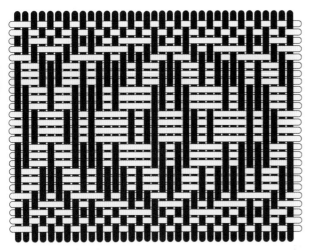

Using Perle No. 12 thread, this weave covers a height of 14mm (approx. ½in), with the length being as wide as you need.

WARP	WEFT
Colour 1 (14mm (approx. ½in) in stitches)	2 x colour 1 21 x colour 2 2 x colour 1

Colour 1

» **1** U1, O1

» **2** O1, U1

Colour 2

» **3** (U1) O2, U4, O1, U1, O4, U2, O1, U2, O4, U1, O1, U4, O2, U1

» **4** (O2, U2) O1, U1, O4, U1, O1, U2, O3, U2, O1, U1, O4, U1, O1, U2, O3, U2, O1, U2, O4, U1, O1, U4, O2, U1, O2, U4, O1, U1, O4, U2

» **5** *(U2) O2, U1, O1, U4, O1, U1, O2, U3, O2, U1, O1, U4, O1, U1, O2, U3*

» **6** Repeat * to *

» **7** Repeat * to *

» **8** #(U1) O2, U4, O1, U1, O4, U2, O1, U2, O4, U1, O1, U4, O2, U1#

» **9** Repeat # to #

» **10** Repeat # to #

» **11** «(O2, U2) O1, U1, O4, U1, O1, U2, O3, U2, O1, U1, O4, U1, O1, U2, O3, U2»

» **12** Repeat « to »

» **13** Repeat « to »

» **14** Repeat « to »

» **15** Repeat Row 11 (#)

» **16** Repeat Row 10 (#)

» **17** Repeat Row 9 (#)

» **18** Repeat Row 8 (*)

» **19** Repeat Row 7 (*)

» **20** Repeat Row 6 (*)

» **21** Repeat Row 5

» **22** Repeat Row 4

» **23** Repeat Row 3

Colour 1

» **24** Repeat Row 2

» **25** Repeat Row 1

NO. 12 – BRAIDS & EDGES

WARP
Colour 1
(14mm (approx. ½in) stitches)

WEFT
4 x colour 2
2 x colour 1
2 x colour 1

Using Perle No. 12 thread, this weave covers a height of 14mm (approx. ½in), with the length being as wide as you need.

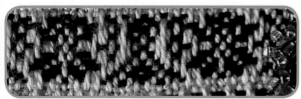

Colour 2

» **1** O2, U2

» **2** O2, U2

» **3** (U2) O2, U2

» **4** (U2) O2, U2

Colour 1

» **5** O1, U1

» **6** (U1) O1, U1

Colour 2

» **7** O1, U2, O1, U5, O1, U3, O1, U2, O1, U2, O1, U3, O1, U2, O1, U2

» **8** (O2, U3) O1, U4, O2, U3, O2, U4, O1, U3, O3, U3

» **9** (U1) O2, U1, O1, U5, O3, U1, O3, U5, O1, U1, O2, U1

» **10** (O2, U1) O1, U3, O3, U1, O2, U1, O2, U1, O3, U3, O1, U1, O3, U1

» **11** O1, U1, O1, U5, O3, U1, O1, U1, O1, U1, O3, U5, O1, U1

» **12** (U1) O1, U3, O1, U3, O3, U1, O1, U1, O3, U3, O1, U3, O1, U1

» **13** O1, U3, O1, U1, O2, U4, O1, U1, O1, U4, O2, U1, O1, U3

» **14–25** Repeat each row in the following order: 12, 11, 10, 9, 8, 7, 6, 5, 4, 3, 2, 1

NO. 13 – BRAIDS & EDGES

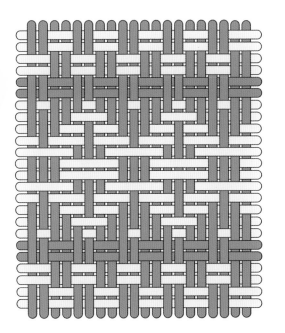

WARP
Colour 1
(14mm (approx. ½in) stitches)
WEFT
Colour 2

Using Perle No. 12 thread, this weave covers a height of 14mm (approx. ½in), with the length being as wide as you need.

» **1** (U2) O2, U2
» **2** (U2) O2, U2
» **3** O2, U2, O2, U2
» **4** (U2) O2, U2
» **5** (U2) O2, U2
» **6** (U1) O1, U3
» **7** (U4) O3, U5
» **8** (U3) O2, U1, O2, U3
» **9** (O1) U1, O3
» **10** (O4) U3, O5
» **11** (U3) O5, U3

» **12** (O4) U3, O5
» **13** (O1) U1, O3
» **14** (U3) O2, U1, O2, U3
» **15** (U4) O3, U5
» **16** (U1) O1, U3
» **17** (U2) O2, U2
» **18** (U2) O2, U2
» **19** O2, U2
» **20** O2, U2
» **21** (U2) O2, U2
» **22** (U2) O2, U2

NO. 14 – BRAIDS & EDGES

WARP
Colour 1
(14mm (approx. ½in) stitches)
WEFT
Colour 2

Using Perle No. 12 thread, this weave covers a height of 14mm (approx. ½in), with the length being as wide as you need.

» **1** (U2) 02, U2

» **2** (U2) 02, U2

» **3** 02, U2

» **4** 02, U2

» **5** (U2) 02, U2

» **6** (U2) 02, U2

» **7** (01) U1, 03

» **8** (U3) 02, U1, 02, U3

» **9** (U4) 03, U5

» **10** (U1) 01, U3

» **11** 03, U5

» **12** (01) U1, 02, U3, 02

» **13** (01, U1) 03, U1

» **14–25** Repeat each row in the following order: 12, 11, 10, 9, 8, 7, 6, 5, 4, 3, 2, 1

TEXTURES

NO.1

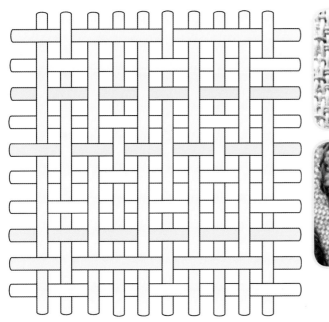

WARP	WEFT	PATTERN REPEAT
Colour 1	Colour 1	Eight rows

- » **1** (U1) O3, U1
- » **2** O1, U3
- » **3** O1, U1
- » **4** (U2) O1, U3
- » **5** (U1) O1, U1
- » **6** (U2) O1, U3
- » **7** O1, U3
- » **8** O1, U1

NO. 2

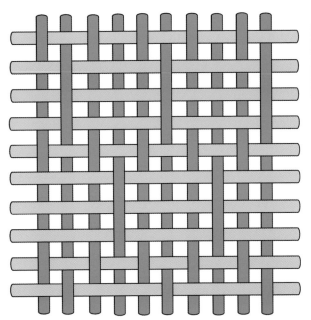

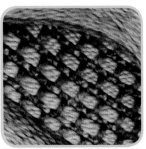

WARP	WEFT	PATTERN REPEAT
Colour 1	Colour 2	Eight rows

- » **1** O1, U1
- » **2** *(U1) O3, U1*
- » **3** Repeat * to *
- » **4** Repeat * to *
- » **5** O1, U1
- » **6** #(O2, U1) O3, U1#
- » **7** Repeat # to #
- » **8** Repeat # to #

NO. 3

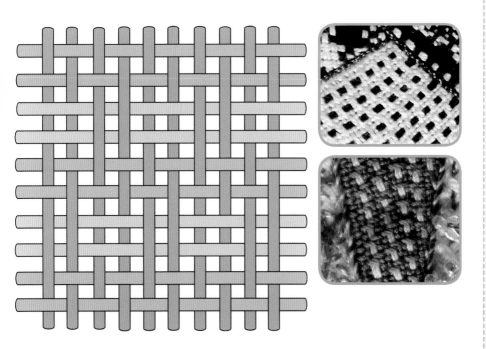

WARP	WEFT	PATTERN REPEAT
Colour 1	Colour 1 Colour 2	Eight rows

Colour 1

» **1**   01, U1
» **2**   (U1) 01, U1

Colour 2

» **3**   02, U2
» **4**   02, U2

Colour 1

» **5**   01, U1
» **6**   (U1) 01, U1

Colour 2

» **7**   U2) 02, U2
» **8**   (U2) 02, U2

NO. 4

WARP	WEFT	PATTERN REPEAT
Colour 1	Colour 2	Eleven rows

- » **1** *O1, U3*
- » **2** Repeat * to *
- » **3** #(U1) O3, U1#
- » **4** Repeat # to #
- » **5** Repeat # to #
- » **6** Repeat * to *
- » **7** Repeat * to *
- » **8** Repeat * to *
- » **9** Repeat # to #
- » **10** Repeat # to #
- » **11** Repeat # to #

NO. 5

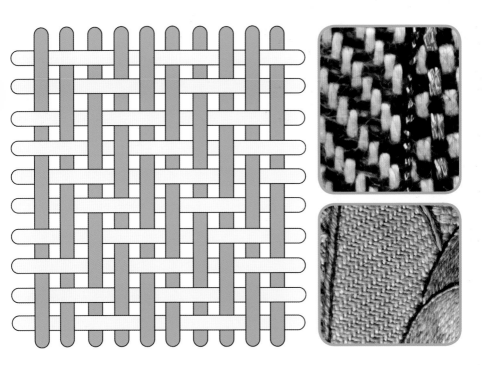

WARP	WEFT	PATTERN REPEAT
Colour 1	Colour 2	Four rows

- » **1**   (O1, U2) O2, U2
- » **2**   (U2) O2, U2
- » **3**   (U1) O2, U2
- » **4**   O2, U2

NO. 6

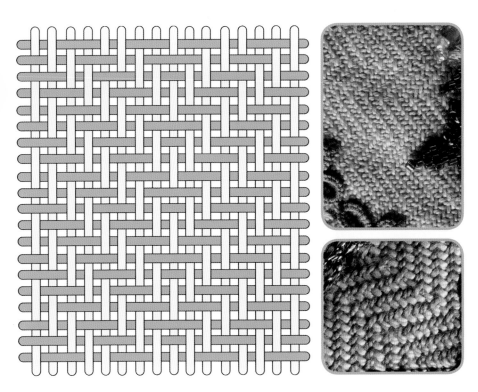

WARP	WEFT	PATTERN REPEAT
Colour 1	Colour 2	Sixteen rows

» **1**   (O1, U2) O2, U2

» **2**   O2, U2

» **3**   (U1) O2, U2

» **4**   (U2) O2, U2

» **5**   (O1, U2) O2, U2

» **6**   O2, U2

» **7**   (U1) O2, U2

» **8**   (U2) O2, U2

» **9**   (O1, U2) O2, U2

» **10** (U2) O2, U2

» **11** (U1) O2, U2

» **12** O2, U2

» **13** (O1, U2) O2, U2

» **14** (U2) O2, U2

» **15** (U1) O2, U2

» **16** O2, U2

NO. 7

WARP	WEFT	PATTERN REPEAT
Colour 1	Colour 2	Six rows

- » **1** (U2) O2, U2
- » **2** (U2) O2, U2
- » **3** (U1) O1, U3
- » **4** O2, U2
- » **5** O2, U2
- » **6** O1, U3

NO. 8

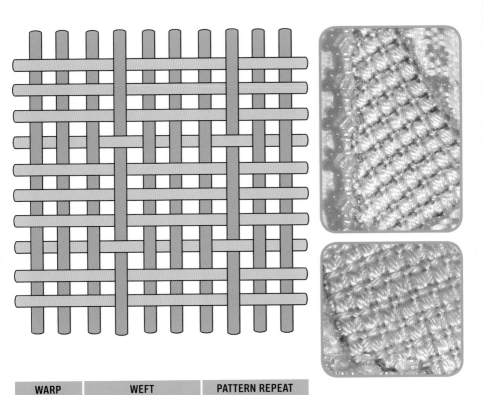

WARP	WEFT	PATTERN REPEAT
Colour 1	Colour 1	Four rows

- » **1** (U3) O1, U3
- » **2** (U3) O1, U3
- » **3** (U3) O1, U3
- » **4** O3, U1

NO. 9

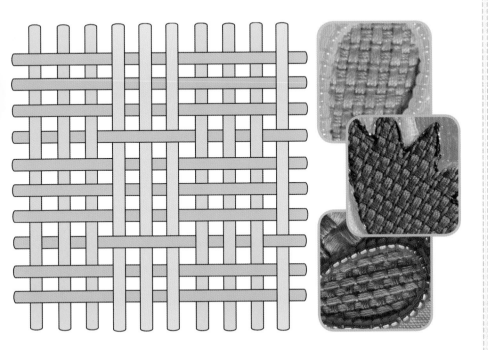

WARP	WEFT	PATTERN REPEAT
Colour 1	Colour 1 or 2	Six rows

- » **1** (U3) O1, U3
- » **2** (U3) O1, U3
- » **3** (U3) O1, U3
- » **4** O3, U1
- » **5** O3, U1
- » **6** O3, U1

NO. 10

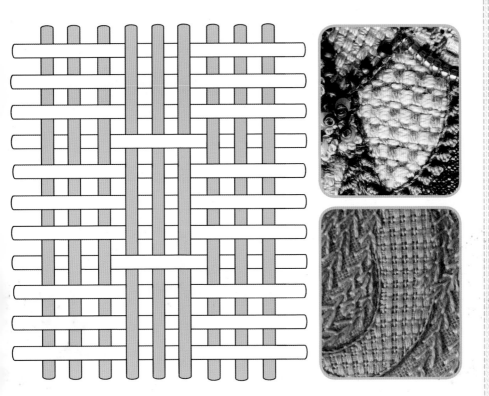

WARP	WEFT	PATTERN REPEAT
Colour 1	Colour 1 or 2	Four rows

» **1**   O3, U3
» **2**   O3, U3
» **3**   O3, U3
» **4**   U3, O3